DEALING WITH IDIOTS

16 Effective Strategies For Dealing With Idiots And Coping With Jerks At Work

Thomas Williams

Thomas Williams

COPYRIGHT © 2022 Thomas Williams.

All rights reserved. No part of this book may be reproduced by mechanical, photographic, or electronic means, or in phonograph form; Nor may they be stored in any downloading system, transmitted, or otherwise copied for public or private use other than "fair use" in the form of short quotations in articles and reviews without the prior written consent of the editor.

TABLE OF CONTENTS

INTRODUCTION 3
16 EFFECTIVE TIPS FOR DEALING WITH IDIOTS AND JERKS 6
   Tip #1: 6
   Tip #2: 7
   Tip #3: 7
   Tip #4: 8
   Tip #5: 9
   Tip #6: 10
   Tip #7: 11
   Tip #8: 12
   Tip #9: 13
   Tip #10 14
   Tip #11: 15
   Tip #12: 16
   Tip #13: 18
   Tip #14: 19
   Tip #15: 20
   Tip #16: 20
DEALING WITH IDIOTS AT WORK 22

INTRODUCTION

Have you ever dealt with people who are always trying to prove their points, no matter how cliché their statements are? Have you ever had a debate with someone that turned into an argument, have you ever tried to talk to people who end up frustrating you, have you ever heard the phrase: *"NEVER ARGUE WITH AN IDIOT"?*

Because dealing with idiots is the most common source of stress nowadays; dealing with idiots can cause you to lose your cool and become irritated. I'm not just talking about those clueless people who have no idea what's going on around them or in this world, who don't know the difference between right and wrong, but also about idiots who always consider themselves superior, talking about idiots who lack the decency to act like a human being.

Dealing with idiots can be very stressful because idiots never think they are wrong, idiots always try

Dealing With Idiots

to prove themselves right without listening to one's valid logic and facts, idiots never listen, they just argue, idiots feel superior and the rest is their inferior, idiots can trade very low and you cannot go to their level, as **Obama** said: *"when idiots go low, you go high"*. but sometimes dealing with idiots can make us so frustrated that we lose our composure and act immorally.

This world has intelligent, logical, and wise people, but not everyone in the world has common sense and wisdom, this world also has idiots who will never give a chance to test your patience, at any moment you can put yourself in a find situation where you can end up dealing with idiots, whether you are traveling or at work, going to school, enjoying your vacation or using a social site, you can always find yourself in a situation where you are dealing with idiots you have.

Therefore, you must learn to deal with idiots without losing calm, you must never let an idiot ruin your day or your life, always remain calm and sensible, and always act wisely.

Have you ever noticed why you're frustrated at work, it's not the wall or the windows or the desk that's irritating you, it's the idiots you work with, the idiots you annoy, the idiots who frustrate you in your workplace. Idiots in any situation, so it's necessary to learn some tips to master the skill of dealing with idiots.

This book will teach you how to deal with those annoying idiots in your home, office, or school. We will present 16 different methods for dealing with idiots and getting them out of your life.

16 Effective Tips For Dealing With Idiots And Jerks

There are so many idiots and jerks that it can be difficult to keep your cool.

Here are some survival tips to help you through the swamp.

Tip #1: Set The Rules

I will say it bluntly:

You must prevent them from dominating conversations and situations. When an ignorant or unkind person discovers they can take advantage of you, they will till you curse the day you ever gave them credit. Idiots and bastards coined the phrase: give an inch and they take a mile. You can't relax too much with these people.

If you have seen someone behaving very rudely, stupidly, or in any way brash and abusive, beware!

Don't promote them at work or invite them out on a date with your sister. Be cautious! They show you who they are.

Tip #2: Give Yourself An Upgrade

The bad and the stupid are energy leeches. They give you endless opportunities to waste your time, energy, and mental effort. But you're not getting anywhere!

So, what can you do to deal with idiots and stupid people?

Start with yourself. Stop looking for external solutions to organize your life, because deep down you know it doesn't work. And that is because you will never find the fulfillment and satisfaction you seek until you look within and unleash your power.

Tip #3: Help Them

One of the best tricks in dealing with idiots and jerks is to help them.

I know it sounds crazy, but stupidity and aggressive behavior are often the results of someone feeling helpless or frustrated.

They help with a sudden awakening.

They feel ashamed and ashamed of their deviant behavior and begin to respect you. It also doesn't have to be anything extravagant...

Perhaps you can teach a highly-annoying coworker Excel or show a guy who can't say a sentence without saying "fuck" every second word how to install a super beneficial program.

Tip #4: Be Wise

Some idiots and jerks have never presented themselves otherwise.

Tell them why they're wrong, in the least personal way. Let them know how their actions, words, or behavior are misleading people. You may be completely unaware of this.

For example, people who think they are always right often act out of a deep sense of insecurity.

If you communicate with them empathically and let them know how others may misinterpret their words, they will often stop and think about what you are saying.

Make it clear that there is nothing personal against them; rather, it is a concern about how others may interpret their behavior and actions. Also, give them an idea or goal to work towards and make sure you can improve a lot as well.

Tip #5: Silence Is Golden

Sometimes the best answer to an idiot is nothing at all. Speaking is easily misunderstood, and everyone understands that actions speak louder than words. People who aren't particularly bright or have a bad attitude have a tendency to disregard what others say.

That's why it's sometimes best not to say anything at all. If they make a bad joke or look at you angrily and insult you, pretend you don't notice them anymore. Go about your day. Their behavior stems from losing your attention, the most valuable currency they covet.

Tip #6: Light Things Up With A Joke

For a reason, humor is the universal language: it works. Once people laugh, they forget the action they are trying to play and all the games they are playing.

You open up for a second to the magic of the moment and become humanized. Look at what they find funny and try to build on that.

It can be a lot of fun, and sometimes you even see a side of that annoying person you didn't know existed. Humor can be the key that opens the door.

That's why sometimes telling a good joke is the best response to dealing with idiots and jerks.

In any case, you can present your material to a difficult audience.

Tip #7: Avoid Them Physically

Sometimes the simplest solution is the best solution. Don't torment yourself if you're dealing with people who've driven you insane with their idiocy and horror.

Simply avoid them physically; it may sound silly, but it works. You value your time more than wasting it on poisonous and ignorant individuals, therefore give them a wide distance. Sometimes it's just not worth it... I'm not suggesting hiding in a broom closet when they come up, but don't answer their calls. Leave their messages there... nod to them when you see them in town, but tell them to be somewhere when they start talking to you.

"Staying within 25 feet of a toxic person means your chances of catching and clearing the disease are more than doubled."

Tip #8: Be As Patient As Possible

There will be situations at work, in your family, or even in your love life where you may be dealing with jerks and idiots with no easy or near exit. You just have to cross the idiot.

In this case, I strongly advise having a thick skin and being patient.

See it as a meditation on human madness. They talk and you smile sweetly and sit back and go about your day as best you can.

Some people are idiots simply because they aren't intelligent in the way that matters to you at the time. For this reason, there are often when the patience of a saint is the best thing you can do.

Tip #9: Look In The Mirror

I'm not saying you're an idiot; I'm guilty of it too, but I believe it's critical that we avoid being a pot calling the kettle black when dealing with idiots and assholes. It's easy to get frustrated in different situations and notice how unfulfilling and ridiculous everyone around us is.

But what about us?

Remember the last time you did something really stupid.

Then try to forgive yourself and the stupid people around you if they're only wrong once or twice.

Nobody is perfect.

"While blaming unethical or inept coworkers may seem easier and safer in the near term, it is simply not a useful story for us to tell."

It's a distortion of reality that can undermine our decisions and alienate our teams.

Tip #10: Get Them Off Their Butt

One of the best remedies for shock and idiocy is motivation.

There are times when you can be a cheerleader and help the asses heal by making them energetic and uplifted. Sometimes the best way to deal with people who hold their heads high is to get them off their butts.

In a work environment, this can mean setting both proactive and critical goals.

In a circle of friends, that might mean encouraging a naughty or stupid friend to work on a goal they've thought about, but you're reluctant to try.

In a family situation, that might mean thinking about home improvement projects or other things you and your family can do to bond. If there are people you can't stand, think about motivating them to become better people.

Anything is achievable if you start small and dream big.

Tip #11: Turn Them

I alluded to this before when I mentioned that sometimes the greatest strategy for dealing with idiots and jerks is to help them.

You defuse a situation by enlisting the help of an idiot or jerk. It's like having a lovely umbrella on a hot day because their asshole vibes stop being focused on you.

Also, their stupidity no longer affects you because they now know that they won't bother you with stupid questions or complaints. You achieve a win-win scenario just by befriending them.

Think of the idiot or jerk as an enemy spy:

You entice them with rewards and positive feedback for being part of your team and encourage them to ignore their horrible behavior around you. It can work.

As Art Markman writes:

"The trick is to make that person an ally. Conscientious people in any workplace are great because they make sure things get done."

Try to get their help and support for the productive activities you do at work.

"Getting them involved in working through the specifics of a project allows them to put their attention to detail to good use while also keeping them too busy to nitpick."

Tip #12: Think About The Context

Some folks are jerks at work but the nicest people you've ever met when you visit them for a Saturday BBQ.

Let's just be honest, leaving aside the more unsettling and schizoid parts of that, and what it says about modern capitalism and labor, some monsters can be created by context.

Nobody is fully one thing or the other, so paying attention to their natural habitat is one of the greatest methods to deal with idiots and jerks. For example, you don't want to see me while I'm hungry. I'm the biggest jerk on the face of the planet.

If you notice what brings inner stupidity and shock to people around you, you can prevent them in those situations and sometimes work to help them overcome those situations or move on.

As Eric Schwitzgebel says:

"Nobody is a perfect jerk or a perfect lover.

"Human behavior - of course! - varies a lot depending on the context. Various situations (sales team meetings, nearby trips) can highlight the excitement of one and the love of another."

Tip #13: Be Better Than Them

Life is not a competition, but it also plays no favorites.

In most situations, the more competent person wins.

Rather than competing, arguing, or clashing with idiots and jerks, simply be better than them.

You'll eventually triumph, whether at your job or in your personal life.

Furthermore, if their behavior has irritated you, you can bet that it has irritated others as well. Jerks and fools rarely make mistakes only once.

They generally have a long list of people who hate them hate. Be better than them and surpass them in your work and actions. It will ultimately serve you well when people get tired of their antiques.

Tip #14: Be prepared for stupidity

If you travel the world and expect to talk to Nobel Prize winners and ethics professors, you will be very disappointed!

There are many of us simple and failed struggling people here on the dirty streets, and we are not always the nicest or most honest people you have ever met. Therefore, you must be ready for stupidity.

For I can guarantee that stupidity will come your way, find you and ruin your day sooner or later.

Just like there are a certain number of raccoons and deer in your neighborhood, there are a certain number of jerks and idiots out there.

You're going to see one eventually. They may even do something to annoy you or endanger your safety.

"However, those are simply the odds." So be prepared. Take care. And don't get too worked up."

Tip #15: Feed Them, Honey

One of the most effective ways to treat jerks is to give them honey. Treat them like they are the best person you've ever met.

Give them sarcastic praises that they will appreciate. Let them be confused and spiritually destroyed by your gentleness. Give them nothing but love and appreciation. If they expect to be scolded and insulted, tell them they are a very "thoughtful" person.

Where they make awful remarks, keep telling them you're "always interested in how they see things."

Give them ideas they can pursue.

Tip #16: Tell Them To Get Lost

Part of building your strength is drawing lines that you won't cross. As well as borders that no one else crosses.

There are idiots and jerks in our world who are really emotional - and sometimes even physical - predators. If you've had to deal with this and you've already tried everything, sometimes you have no choice but to tell them to stop.

Sometimes idiots and jerks just need to be confronted and told to hum.

You may feel like a bad person, but if you've already tried other strategies and done your best, that might be all you need to try. Put your foot down and kick hard.

Let them know you've had enough and you've got better things to do. Tell them it's nothing personal, just that you're busy and don't have time to talk or do what they're talking about.

If they want to argue, tell them you're not interested, that you're done with their behavior, and move on. It's easy.

Dealing With Idiots At Work

"One of the most effective ways to cope with a toxic person at work is to treat them like a toxic substance."

Dealing with an idiot at work aka ID-10-T Why can idiots at work drive away your best employees? How would you describe a person with a bad or negative attitude? can you do something about it Stop and ask yourself these questions and are they affecting you and your work team?

Most likely, they are present in your work environment and whether the asshole bothers you or not, they will probably bother one of the team members. If you're the boss and your natural style isn't hampered by theirs, then your usual reaction is to just ignore the situation and tell others they're just ignoring it and forgetting about it. It might be the worst thing a leader can do, but it happens all the time. By doing nothing, you encourage (essentially reward) the behavior and discriminate against better team members. After enough of this, the best will get frustrated and start looking elsewhere. Yes, this strategy works.

Let's stop and analyze negative attitudes and negative behaviors.

Before you can stop and analyze the negative attitude or behavior, take a blank sheet of paper and draw a line down the middle. Write the title "Positive Attitudes" at the top of the right column and the title "Negative Attitudes" at the top of the left column. Start in the right column, noting the traits and behaviors you notice in people with positive attitudes. It should be easy. Your list will likely include improved team morale, increased productivity, reduced absenteeism, and petty gossip, among many others. Go ahead and do it now.

Do the same in the left column with the negative settings. If you're like most people, this column contains the opposite of what you have in the right column.

That might not surprise you, would it? The real secret is to do it with a group, and the most effective way is to split the group in half. Divide them into two different pieces before you begin. Do not talk to them about the exercise until they are in separate rooms.

Give one group the positive and the other group the negative. Be sure and don't show that the other group has the opposite. This works especially well if each group has a large flipchart to record responses on.

When they have finished the exercise, which should take no more than 15 minutes, bring them back together and ask one speaker from each group to read what they have written. What do you think will happen next time they meet?

The real secret of all exercises is debriefing. Don't skip this section and don't worry if it takes 30-45 minutes. Asking everyone's opinion on the importance of this benefits the whole team, including those who are already positive.

If possible, post the negative and positive comments on a bulletin board after the debrief for everyone to see. The memory factor is excellent. Don't be afraid to bring up the subject in regular employee reviews. The more you discuss attitudes and behaviors, the more effective the communication between the team will be. As communication improves, productivity increases, and as productivity increases, smiles and bad attitudes decrease.

Printed in Great Britain
by Amazon